THE HUMAN MACHINE

RESPIRATION AND CIRCULATION

Louise Spilsbury

© 2008 Heinemann Library
a division of Reed Elsevier Inc.
Chicago, Illinois

Customer Service 888-454-2279
Visit our website at www.heinemannraintree.com

Designed by Victoria Bevan and AMR Design Ltd
Illustrations by Medi-mation
Picture Research by Hannah Taylor

Originated by Chroma
Printed and bound in China by CTPS

12 11 10 09 08
10 9 8 7 6 5 4 3 2 1

**Library of Congress Cataloging-in-Publication
Data**

Spilsbury, Louise.
  Respiration and circulation / Louise Spilsbury.
    p. cm. -- (The human machine)
  Includes index.
  ISBN-13: 978-1-4329-0907-9 (hardback : alk.
paper)
  ISBN-13: 978-1-4329-0914-7 (pbk. : alk. paper)
  1. Respiration--Juvenile literature. 2. Blood--
Circulation--Juvenile literature. I. Title.
  QP121.S725 2007
  612.2--dc22
                                    2007031963

Acknowledgments
The publishers would like to thank the following
for permission to reproduce photographs: ©Alamy
pp. **14** (Ana Maria Marques), **16** (Phototake Inc);
©Corbis pp. **4** (Peter Barrett), **21** (Roy Morsch),
23 (zefa/ Hein van den Heuvel); ©Getty Images
pp. **25** (AFP/ Stan Honda), **26** (Photodisc), **27**
(Photodisc/ Karl Weatherly), **18** (Stockbyte), **9**
(Stone), **5** (Taxi), **24** (Travelpix Ltd.); ©iStockphoto
p. **29** (Justin Horrocks); ©Photolibrary pp. **7**
(Corbis Corporation), **22** (Digital Vision), **13** (Flirt);
©Science Photo Library pp. **11** (AJ Photo), **17**
(National Cancer Institute), **28** (Roger Harris),
19 (Steve Gschmeissner).

Cover photograph of the heart and lungs
reproduced with permission of ©Science Photo
Library/ Hybrid Medical Animation.

The publishers would like to thank David Wright
for his assistance in the preparation of this book.

Every effort has been made to contact copyright
holders of any material reproduced in this book.
Any omissions will be rectified in subsequent
printings if notice is given to the publishers.

Contents

Any words appearing in the text in bold, **like this**, are explained in the glossary.

What Are Respiration and Circulation?

The human body is often compared to a complex machine because it is made up of different parts that are linked together to make it work. Like other machines, the human body needs **energy** for everything it does, from sleeping to swimming. The **respiratory system** and the **circulatory system** are body systems that help the human machine to release this energy.

Breathe in!

To make energy, our bodies need two substances—food and **oxygen**. Oxygen is a gas in the air. The body needs oxygen to release energy from the food we eat. It takes oxygen into the lungs by breathing. We breathe all the time, day and night, to take in a constant supply of oxygen. Taking air in and out of the body and using it to release energy from our food is called respiration.

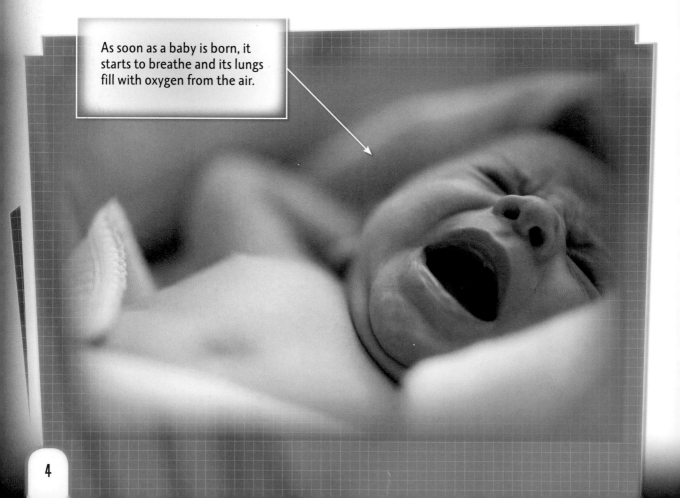

As soon as a baby is born, it starts to breathe and its lungs fill with oxygen from the air.

The circulatory system

The food and the oxygen used to release energy are transported around the body by the blood. Blood circulates, or travels around, through the body's network of **blood vessels** (tubes). It collects oxygen from the lungs and drops it off where it is needed. Blood also delivers food that has been **digested** around the body. Digested food is food that the body has broken down into a form it can use. The way blood travels around the body, transporting important substances, is called circulation.

When you are active, your body requires more energy than it does when you are resting.

HEAT AND ENERGY

Lizards and other cold-blooded animals have bodies that change temperature depending on the temperature of their surroundings. Warm-blooded animals, such as humans, keep a constant body temperature. To do this we must produce a lot of energy. That is why we need to eat regularly. Humans also have big lungs to get the oxygen we need to produce plenty of energy.

How Do We Breathe?

Pumps are machines that push air in or out. In the human machine there are several different parts that help us to breathe. We take air into our mouth and throat by sucking it up through the mouth and nose. From the throat, the air goes into the **trachea**, a long tube that runs down to the chest. There are two large tubes called **bronchi** at the bottom of the trachea. One of the bronchi carries air into the left lung, while the other carries air into the right lung.

Looking at the lungs

Your lungs are the body's oxygen tanks. They take up most of the space in your chest. An adult's lungs can hold about 10 pints (6 liters) of air, but they usually take in about half that with each breath. You usually breathe about 15 times a minute, or nearly 25,000 times a day!

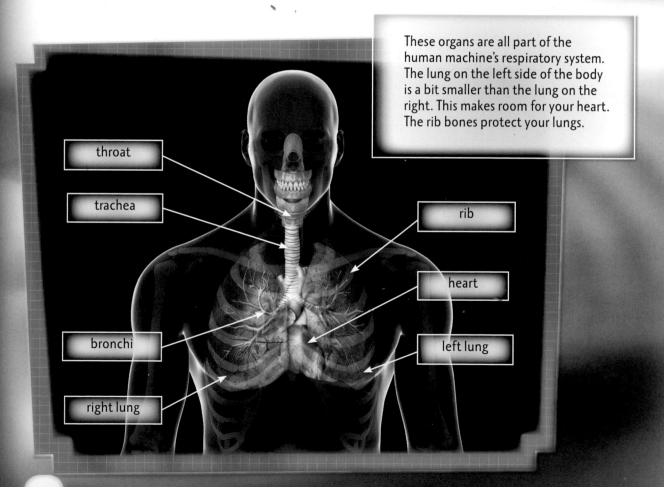

These organs are all part of the human machine's respiratory system. The lung on the left side of the body is a bit smaller than the lung on the right. This makes room for your heart. The rib bones protect your lungs.

throat

trachea

rib

heart

bronchi

left lung

right lung

Knowing about the nose

We mostly breathe in through the nose. Air moves through the nose to a space called the nasal cavity, which is behind the nose. From there it moves into the back of the throat and on to the trachea. Your lungs could be damaged by dirt or dust, so your nose also works like a filtering machine. It is lined with hairs and a sticky liquid called **mucus**. These trap dirt in the air that you breathe in so that you can blow them out again.

People cannot survive without air for longer than a few minutes. In order to stay underwater for longer, divers have to carry tanks of oxygen with them.

WHY DO I SNEEZE?

A sneeze clears the upper parts of the respiratory system, such as the trachea, to get rid of extra mucus, dust, or other bits of dirt. A sneeze can blast air out at about 100 miles (160 kilometers) an hour—which is as fast as a speeding train!

How do the lungs work?

Air is forced in and out of your lungs by movements of your **diaphragm**. The diaphragm is a band of muscle that lies between your stomach and your lungs. To breathe in, your diaphragm **contracts**, which means it tightens and flattens. At the same time, muscles attached to the ribs move the ribs upward and outward. This makes the chest bigger. As this happens, air is sucked into the trachea to inflate the lungs with air.

To exhale, or breathe out, this process is reversed. Your diaphragm relaxes and moves up. Your rib muscles relax and the rib cage lowers. These actions work to push air out of the lungs. You can feel your lungs working if you hold your chest when you breathe in and out.

Like a constantly working pump, the chest expands to suck air into the lungs and compresses (gets smaller) to push air out again.

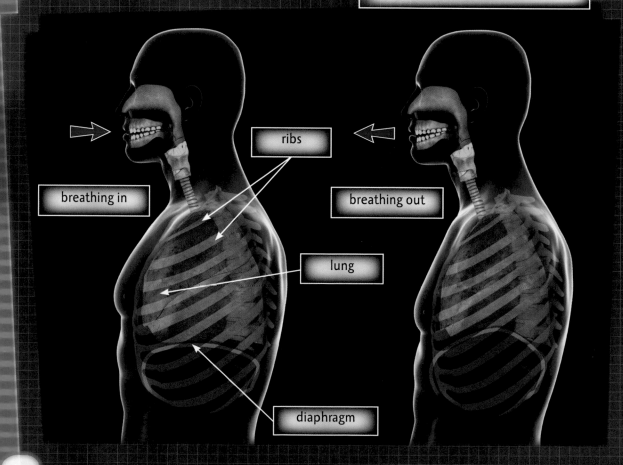

ribs

breathing in

breathing out

lung

diaphragm

How do lungs know when to breathe?

Some machines are controlled by a central computer. In the human machine, the brain controls our breathing so that we do not have to think about it. Breathing is an involuntary action. It is controlled by a part of the brain called the medulla. The medulla sends signals to the body to keep us breathing in and out about once every five seconds!

Sometimes we control our breathing voluntarily. For example, we can hold our breath for a few minutes when we swim underwater. After a short time the involuntary control takes over and makes us breathe normally again.

A foot pump works in a similar way to lungs. The pump expands when full of air. It then releases air (into the bed) when you push down on it, making the air space smaller. Lungs expand to fill with air and reduce in size to push out air.

WHAT ARE HICCUPS?

Hiccups are when your diaphragm contracts suddenly and jerks abruptly. This makes you swallow a sharp intake of breath that causes the hiccup sound. Hiccups sometimes happen if you have eaten your food too quickly and swallowed too much air.

Inside the lungs

After the air has entered your lungs through the tubes called bronchi, it passes into narrower and shorter tubes called **bronchioles**. These grow out of the bronchi like the branches and twigs on a tree trunk. There are about 30,000 bronchioles in each lung, and some are as thin as a human hair!

Alveoli

At the ends of each of the smallest bronchioles there are clusters of tiny sacs, or bags, called **alveoli**. The air passes along the bronchioles and into the alveoli. They fill up with air so that they look a bit like tiny balloons. Each of the spongy alveoli has a network of very small blood vessels, called **capillaries**, wrapped around it.

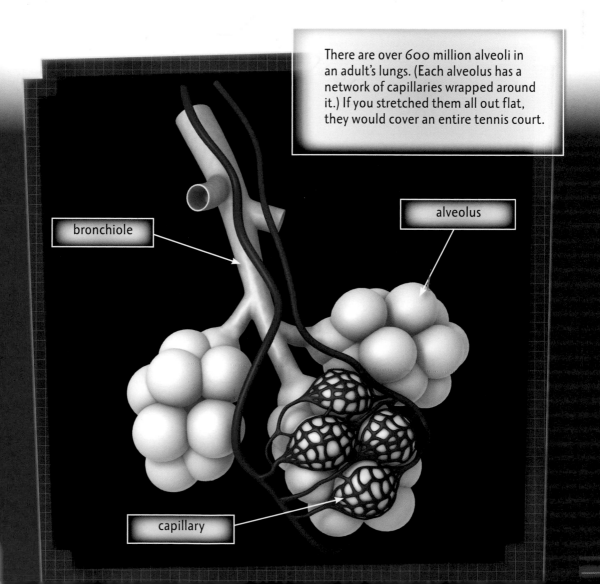

There are over 600 million alveoli in an adult's lungs. (Each alveolus has a network of capillaries wrapped around it.) If you stretched them all out flat, they would cover an entire tennis court.

bronchiole

alveolus

capillary

Diffusion

The walls of the alveoli and the capillaries around them are incredibly thin. Oxygen passes from the alveoli into the capillaries through these walls by **diffusion**. This happens because there is more oxygen in the alveoli than in the blood. The oxygen passes into the blood to try to balance out the different amounts. Oxygen keeps moving from the alveoli into the blood because we are constantly breathing in more oxygen. The blood then carries the oxygen around the body in the circulatory system.

People who have breathing problems caused by the condition called asthma may use inhalers. Inhalers help them breathe in medicines that open up the bronchi and bronchioles again.

WHAT IS ASTHMA?

Asthma is a condition that irritates the bronchi and bronchioles, making them contract so that air cannot be easily breathed in. The bronchi also swell and produce extra mucus. The mucus makes it harder for air to get in and out of the lungs. That is why people with asthma sometimes have difficulty breathing.

How Does Circulation Work?

The blood is the human body's delivery service. It carries oxygen from the alveoli inside the lungs all over the body. Cars and many other machines have pumps to move fuel to where it is needed. In the human machine the heart is the pump that pushes blood around the body, to deliver oxygen to the **cells**.

The heart

Blood moves from the lungs, where it is filled with oxygen, to the heart. The heart lies in the middle of the chest, on the left-hand side of the body. It is about the size of a clenched fist. The heart is divided into four hollow sections. The upper two sections are called atria. (A single section is called an **atrium**.) They are joined to the two lower sections called **ventricles**.

The heart is a pump made of cardiac muscle. Unlike other types of muscle, cardiac muscle never gets tired.

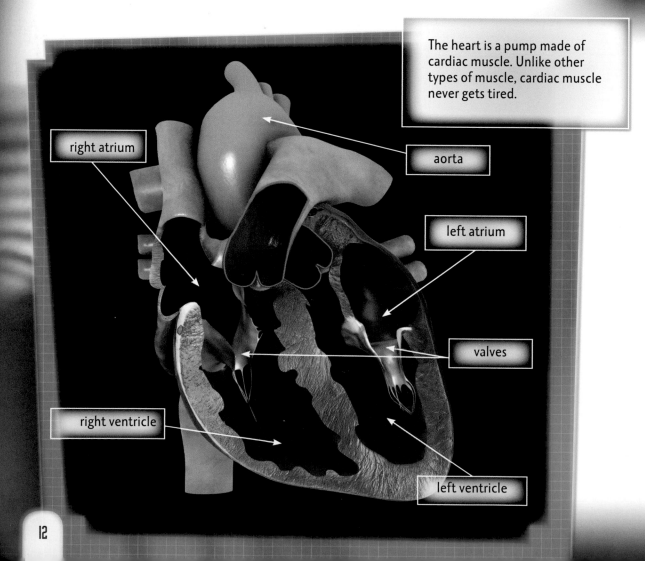

right atrium

aorta

left atrium

valves

right ventricle

left ventricle

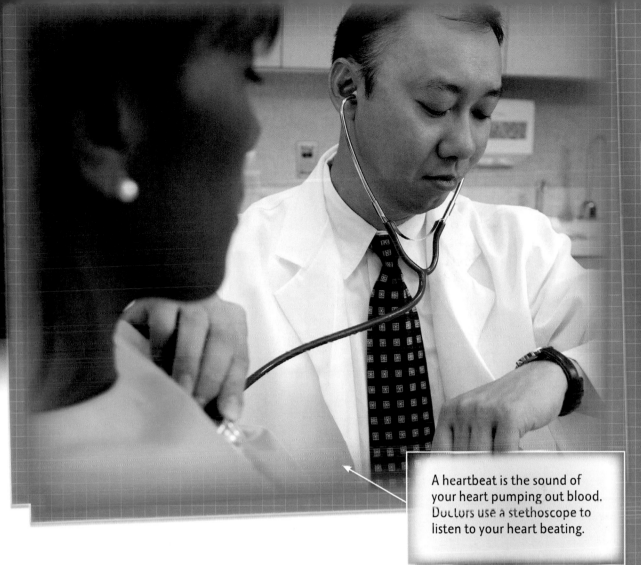

A heartbeat is the sound of your heart pumping out blood. Doctors use a stethoscope to listen to your heart beating.

Blood in the heart

When oxygen-rich blood from the lungs enters the left atrium of the heart, it goes through a one-way **valve** into the left ventricle. The valve acts like a trapdoor that stops blood from flowing the wrong way. When it leaves the heart, blood passes from the left ventricle into the **aorta**. The aorta is the blood vessel that carries blood out of the heart to begin its journey around the rest of the body.

KEEPING YOUR HEART HEALTHY

Your heart is a muscle. Like other muscles in the body, you need to exercise it to keep it strong. Your heart beats more often when you exercise, sending more oxygen and **nutrients** to the muscles to give them energy. Regular exercise makes your heart work more efficiently, so that it can pump more blood with each beat.

How many times does a heart beat?

An adult heart beats, or pumps, about 70 times a minute. Before each beat, your heart fills with blood. When the heart muscles contract, they squeeze the heart to force the blood out into the blood vessels. Between beats the heart relaxes and fills with blood again.

Where does the blood go?

The blood circulates around the whole body through an intricate system of blood vessels. When blood returns to the heart, it passes into the right atrium and ventricle. From there it is pumped into the lungs to get a fresh supply of oxygen. From the lungs, blood goes back to the left side of the heart, and the heart pumps it out to start its journey all over again.

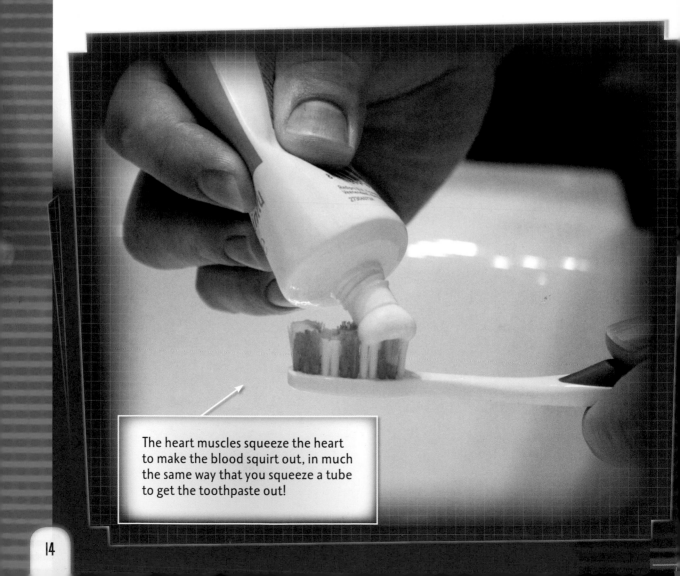

The heart muscles squeeze the heart to make the blood squirt out, in much the same way that you squeeze a tube to get the toothpaste out!

Different blood vessels

If you laid out an adult's blood vessels in a line, the line would be 100,000 miles (160,000 kilometers) long! Blood traveling away from the heart is carried by blood vessels called **arteries**. Blood traveling back to the heart is carried through **veins**. Muscles in the walls of the arteries and veins squeeze and relax to keep the flow of blood moving smoothly. Tiny blood vessels called capillaries connect the arteries and veins and branch out to reach individual cells.

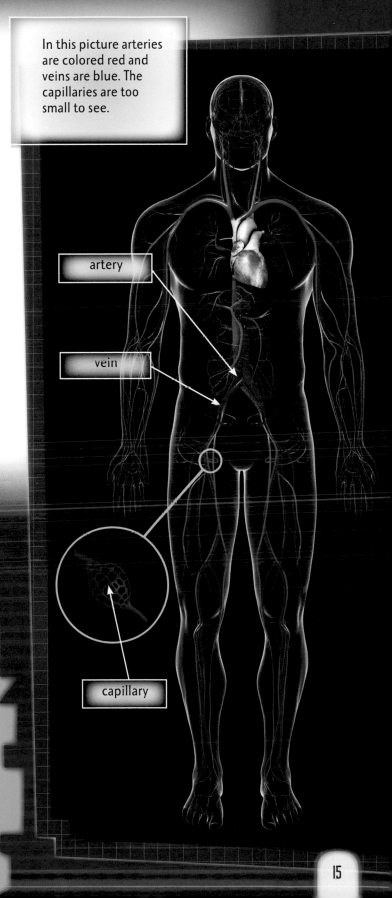

In this picture arteries are colored red and veins are blue. The capillaries are too small to see.

artery

vein

capillary

WHAT ARE CLOGGED ARTERIES?

Eating too many fatty foods, like chocolate, cakes, and chips, can clog your arteries. The fat in foods can build up on the artery walls, allowing less blood to get through. Then the heart has to pump harder to move blood through them. This leads to high blood pressure, which is dangerous.

What Is Blood Made Of?

Our blood is made up of yellowish fluid called plasma and blood cells. Plasma is the liquid part of blood and is mainly water. Floating in the plasma are **red blood cells**, **white blood cells**, and small cell fragments (bits) called **platelets**.

How much blood do we have?

An average man has about 9 to 10 pints (5 to 6 liters) of blood, while a woman has about about 8 pints (4 liters) of blood. The actual amount of blood you have depends on your height and weight. Blood cells can replace themselves when they wear out or are damaged. In fact, more than two million blood cells are replaced every second.

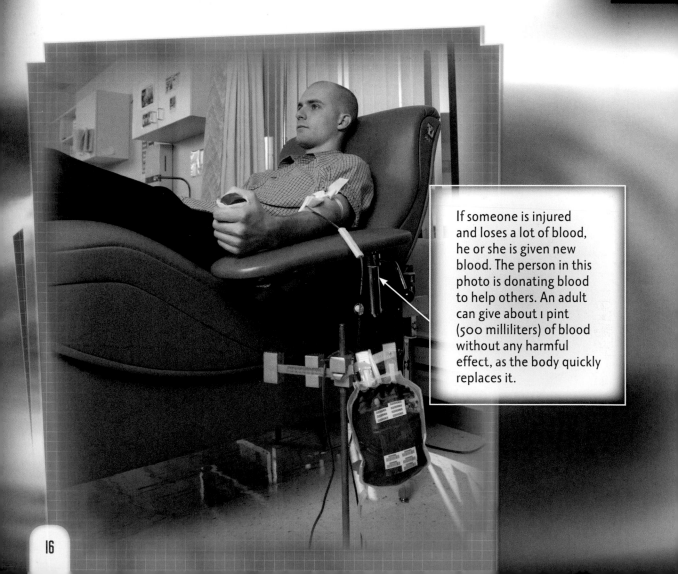

If someone is injured and loses a lot of blood, he or she is given new blood. The person in this photo is donating blood to help others. An adult can give about 1 pint (500 milliliters) of blood without any harmful effect, as the body quickly replaces it.

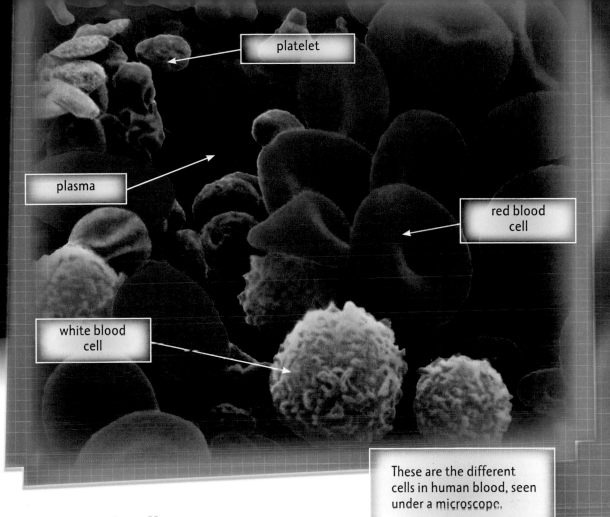

platelet

plasma

red blood cell

white blood cell

These are the different cells in human blood, seen under a microscope.

Red blood cells

Red blood cells are the most common type of blood cell. A single drop of blood contains five million red blood cells! Red blood cells contain a substance called hemoglobin. This is what makes blood look red. Hemoglobin captures oxygen when blood passes through the lungs and then carries it through the bloodstream. If you imagine that the hemoglobin in a red blood cell is like a bus, then oxygen is a passenger on that bus. A single red blood cell travels about 9 miles (15 kilometers) each day.

WHAT IS ANEMIA?

Anemia is when your blood does not have enough hemoglobin. All parts of your body need oxygen to release energy, so someone who is anemic may feel weak and tired. Also, because they do not have enough red hemoglobin, they look paler than normal.

White blood cells

Bacteria are tiny living things that we cannot see. They live inside us and in the world around us. Some of these bacteria can cause infections and diseases. White blood cells help to defend the body by attacking bacteria that get into the blood. Some white blood cells make holes in the walls of bacteria or eat them by releasing substances that break them down.

Some white blood cells make special disease-fighting substances called **antibodies**. Antibodies find and surround the bacteria, making the different bacteria cluster together. This makes it easy for other white blood cells to find and devour them. When pus weeps from an infected wound, it looks yellowy-white because it is mostly made up of white blood cells. These are the worn-out cells that defended the body against the bacteria that caused the infection.

One cubic millimeter of blood usually contains around 7,000 white blood cells. When you are sick, your body makes more white blood cells to fight the disease.

What are platelets?

Platelets are like the human machine's puncture repair kit. If your skin gets cut and you start to bleed, platelets form a clot. They plug up the wound by sticking to it and to each other to stop blood from escaping. The clot cannot hold for long, so platelets also make a stringy protein called fibrin. Fibrin, platelets, and plasma combine to create scabs. These crusty lids prevent dirt and germs from infecting the wound. Once the skin has repaired itself, scabs dry out and fall off. So, remember not to pick scabs—they have an important job to do.

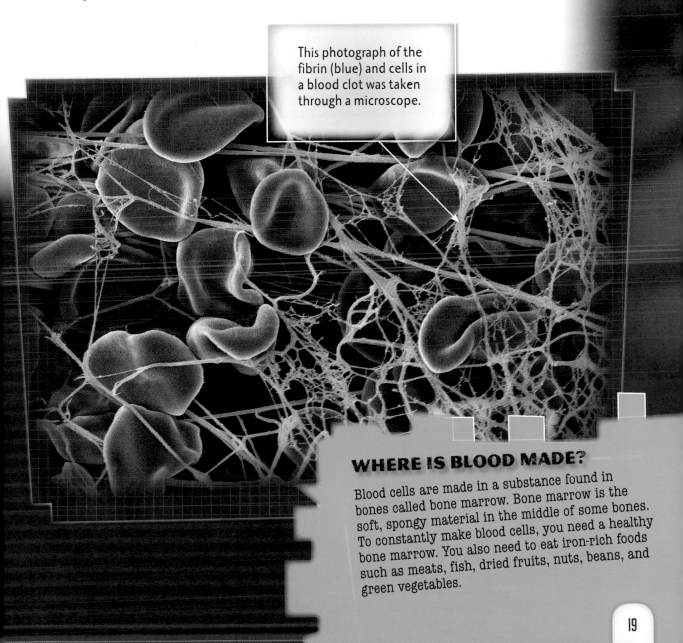

This photograph of the fibrin (blue) and cells in a blood clot was taken through a microscope.

WHERE IS BLOOD MADE?

Blood cells are made in a substance found in bones called bone marrow. Bone marrow is the soft, spongy material in the middle of some bones. To constantly make blood cells, you need a healthy bone marrow. You also need to eat iron-rich foods such as meats, fish, dried fruits, nuts, beans, and green vegetables.

How Do We Get Energy?

A car engine burns gasoline with oxygen to make energy. The human machine uses oxygen and nutrients from the food we eat to release energy. To use food as fuel, the body must first digest it. The stomach and other parts of the **digestive system** break foods down into a watery fluid containing different nutrients. **Glucose** is the main nutrient that is the body's fuel. It is mostly found in carbohydrate foods such as bread, pasta, and potatoes.

Fuel supplies

Every single cell in the body needs energy, so glucose and oxygen must be taken around the body to all the cells. The blood carries oxygen from the lungs and glucose from digested food. Cells are surrounded by a network of tiny capillaries. The cells have less oxygen and glucose than the blood, so oxygen and glucose pass from the capillaries into the cells by the process called diffusion.

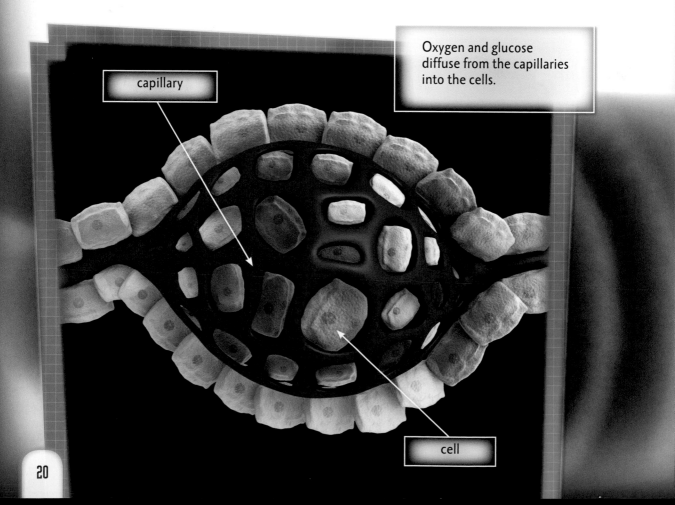

Oxygen and glucose diffuse from the capillaries into the cells.

capillary

cell

Be active! It is important to balance your food intake with your energy output.

Releasing energy

Inside the cells, glucose and oxygen combine in a kind of controlled burning. This is called **aerobic respiration**. This process releases the energy the cells need to make them work. This kind of burning is not like burning in a bonfire— there are no flames. When energy is released in cells it is called "burning" because, as in a bonfire or in a car engine, the process uses oxygen to release energy from a fuel, and it still produces some warmth.

EATING HEALTHY AMOUNTS

When the food we eat contains more energy than our body needs, we store the excess as fat. These fat stores can be used to release energy when we need it. However, if people regularly overeat, they end up with too much fat and become overweight. Being overweight is bad for your heart and can cause other health problems.

Energy and body heat

In a car, the heat energy produced by burning fuel is generally wasted. In the human machine the heat produced by respiration is used to maintain the body's temperature. The outer parts of your body, such as your toes and fingers, may sometimes feel cold, but the core, or central part, of your body usually stays at around 98.6°F (37°C). This is the temperature at which organs inside you, such as the heart and liver, function properly.

When the core of the body gets too cold, one of the ways the human machine tries to keep itself warm is by burning up food at a faster rate. This can cause the body to run out of energy. If the body core gets too hot, vital organs and muscles become overheated and stop working properly.

Respiration provides the heat you need to keep the core of your body warm. You can also wear warmer clothes to keep in your body heat.

Speeding up and slowing down

To make engines go faster or slower, you increase or decrease their power. The human machine works in a similar way. While you are asleep you only use a small amount of energy, so your breathing rate is slow. When you exercise hard your body needs more energy, so you breathe more quickly. This takes more oxygen into the respiratory system. Your heart beats faster, too, increasing the speed at which blood delivers oxygen to the cells.

Blood carries warmth, too. When warm blood comes close to the skin's surface to cool down, it can make people look red in the face.

WHY DO I TURN RED WHEN I RUN?

When you run, the extra heat released by the cells is carried around the body by the blood. To help cool the blood, capillaries carrying blood near the skin's surface can expand, or get wider. This allows more heat to escape into the air. The wider blood vessels can also cause the skin's surface to look red.

Producing waste

When a car uses up fuel to make energy, it produces waste gases that are released as exhaust fumes. When the human machine uses up glucose and oxygen to make energy, the waste products are water and a gas called **carbon dioxide**.

Collecting waste

Waste products are collected from the cells by plasma in the blood as it flows through the circulatory system. At the same time as fresh supplies of nutrients and oxygen diffuse into cells from the blood, waste products diffuse the other way—out of the cells and into the blood. When oxygen-rich blood fresh from the lungs is pumped from the heart, it is bright red. The blood that flows back to the heart has less oxygen and more waste products in it, so it is more of a rusty red color.

Like human machines, the machines in power stations also release waste gases into the air.

Dumping waste

When blood carrying waste from the cells reaches the heart, the heart pumps it straight into the lungs. Within the lungs, carbon dioxide and water diffuse out of the blood and into the alveoli. Then these waste products pass back up the bronchioles, bronchi, and trachea, through the throat, and are breathed out through the nose and mouth.

The respiratory and circulatory systems are essential for life. Without a constant supply of oxygen and nutrients, your cells would not get the energy they need, and the human machine simply could not function.

We also breathe out water vapor when we exhale. On very cold days you can see the water in your breath as a mist in the air.

MISTY BREATH

The water that you exhale with your warm breath is water vapor. This is water in gas form, so usually you cannot see it. On a winter day, the very cold air makes water vapor condense. It turns from a gas into tiny droplets of water. These form a mist in the air.

How Can We Keep Our Heart and Lungs Healthy?

If machines are not used regularly, they can get rusty and stop working properly. In the same way, regular exercise keeps the human machine working well. If machines are given the wrong kind of fuels, they can be damaged. There are also certain things—such as smoking—that are bad for human machines.

What is aerobic exercise?

The best kinds of exercise are the ones you enjoy, but aerobic exercises are especially good for your lungs and heart. "Aerobic" means "needing oxygen," and aerobic exercises are those that make you breathe hard and increase your heart rate. Basically, aerobic exercises, such as running, playing soccer, cycling, and dancing, leave you feeling out of breath! Try to do some aerobic exercise at least two or three times a week for around 30 minutes at a time.

Swimming is an aerobic exercise that keeps your heart and lungs healthy.

Taking your pulse tells you how hard your heart is working. To take your pulse, hold two forefingers of one hand on the inside of the other wrist so that they line up with the thumb on that hand.

Why is smoking bad for me?

Smoking makes it harder to breathe, so it is bad for your whole body. It is especially damaging to your heart and lungs. Cigarette smoke can break down the walls of the alveoli, making it much harder to take oxygen into the blood. Cigarette smoke can also damage the cells of the lungs and cause cancer, a disease that can be deadly. Smoking cigarettes also increases the risk of heart disease. So, be kind to your body and never smoke!

TAKE YOUR PULSE!

Your pulse rate is the number of times your heart beats in a minute. You can feel it as a throbbing in your wrist. Pulse rates vary, but for a child of 10 it is likely to be between 80 and 100 when you are resting. Take your pulse rate before and after exercise and see how it changes.

The World's Most Complex Machine

The human body is often described as the world's most complex machine, but of course it is not really a machine at all. Machines are non-living, mechanical objects, whereas our bodies are natural, living things. But there are similarities. Like a machine, the body is made up of different parts that work together in systems to do particular jobs. These different systems work together to make the whole body—or the human machine—run smoothly and efficiently.

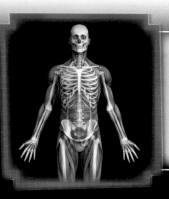

THE SKELETAL SYSTEM

This system of bones supports the other parts of the body, rather like the way the metal frame of a car supports the vehicle.

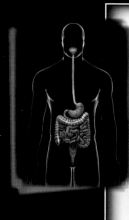

THE DIGESTIVE SYSTEM

The digestive system works as a food-processing machine. It consists of various organs that work together to break down food into forms that the body can use as fuel and raw materials.

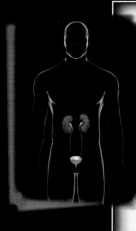

THE EXCRETORY SYSTEM

This is the human machine's waste disposal system, removing harmful substances and waste produced by the other parts of the body.

THE NERVOUS SYSTEM

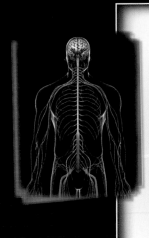

This is the human machine's communication and control system. The brain transmits and receives messages from the senses and the rest of the body. It does this through a network of nerves connected to the brain via the spinal cord.

THE CIRCULATORY SYSTEM

This is the body's delivery system. The heart pumps blood through blood vessels, carrying nutrients and oxygen to the other parts and removing waste from cells.

THE RESPIRATORY SYSTEM

This system provides the rest of the body with the oxygen it needs to get energy from food. It also releases waste gases from the body into the air.

THE MUSCULAR SYSTEM

Muscles are the human machine's motors. Some muscles make the bones of the skeleton move, while others work as pumps to keep substances moving through the body.

Glossary

aerobic respiration process in which oxygen is used to make energy from glucose

alveoli tiny air sacs (bags) at the end of the bronchioles in the lungs

antibody substance that recognizes and helps fight infections and other unwanted substances in the body

aorta main artery that carries blood from the heart to the body

artery blood vessel that carries blood from the heart to the body

atrium upper chamber of the heart where blood collects before passing to the ventricle

bacteria microscopic living thing

blood vessel hollow tube that carries blood in the body

bronchi pair of large air passages that lead from the trachea (windpipe) to the lungs

bronchiole tiny tube that leads from the bronchi to the alveoli in the lungs

capillary smallest kind of blood vessel in the body

carbon dioxide gas found in air that is produced when living things release energy from food

cell building block or basic unit of all living things

circulatory system system that moves blood throughout the body

contract tighten or squeeze

diaphragm band of muscle below the lungs that helps the body breathe in and out

diffusion movement of a substance from an area where there is a lot of it to an area where there is less

digest break down foods we eat into a form that can be absorbed into the blood and used by the body

digestive system parts of the body, such as the stomach and intestines, used in the process of digestion

energy in science, energy is the ability to do work—to move, grow, change, or anything else that living things do

glucose kind of sugar that the body obtains from carbohydrate foods such as pasta and potatoes

mucus slippery, sticky substance produced by some parts of the body such as the nose and throat

nutrient substance that plants and animals need to grow and survive

organ part of the body that performs a specific function

oxygen gas in the air

platelet small cell fragment (bit) in the blood that helps prevent bleeding by causing blood clots to form

red blood cell special type of cell for carrying oxygen in the blood to different parts of the body

respiratory system parts of the body, including the throat and lungs, that take air in and out of the body

trachea tube that carries air to the lungs

valve flap that closes to stops blood from flowing in the wrong direction

vein blood vessel that carries blood from the capillaries toward the heart

ventricle lower chamber of the heart. Blood pumps out of the ventricles to the rest of the body.

white blood cell special type of blood cell that helps the body get rid of unwanted bacteria

Find Out More

Websites

At www.smm.org/heart/lungs/top.html there are animations and activities that deal with the heart and lungs.

At www.nlm.nih.gov/changingthefaceofmedicine/activities/circulatory.html there are interactive information pages about the circulatory system.

At www.kidshealth.org/kid/htbw/heart.html you can learn more about the heart and circulatory system.

Books

Ballard, Carol. *Lungs*. Chicago: Heinemann Library, 2003.

Parker, Steve. *The Heart, Lungs, and Blood*. Chicago: Raintree, 2004.

Parker, Steve. *Pump It Up: Respiration and Circulation*. Chicago: Raintree, 2007.

Simon, Seymour. *Lungs: Your Respiratory System*. New York: Collins, 2007.

Index

Pebble® Plus

SPORTS STARS

STARS OF BASKETBALL

by Matt Doeden

Consulting Editor: Gail Saunders-Smith, PhD

CAPSTONE PRESS
a capstone imprint

Pebble Plus is published by Capstone Press,
1710 Roe Crest Drive, North Mankato, Minnesota 56003
www.capstonepub.com

Library of Congress Cataloging-in-Publication Data
Doeden, Matt.
  Stars of basketball / by Matt Doeden.
    pages cm.—(Pebble plus. Sports stars)
  Includes bibliographical references and index.
  Summary: "Simple text and full-color photographs feature eight current outstanding professional basketball players"—
Provided by publisher.
  ISBN 978-1-4765-3959-1 (library binding)
  ISBN 978-1-4765-6024-3 (ebook PDF)
1. Basketball players—Juvenile literature. I. Title.
  GV885.1.D65 2014
  796.3230922—dc23 [B]   2013030133

Editorial Credits
Erika L. Shores, editor; Sarah Bennett, designer; Eric Gohl, media researcher; Eric Manske, production specialist

Photo Credits
AP Photo: Morry Gash, cover; Newscom: ABACAUSA.COM/Renee Jones Schneider, 17, Cal Sport Media/Anthony Nesmith, 21, Cal Sport Media/Chris Szagola, 9, 11, EPA/David Maxwell, 13, EPA/Rhona Wise, 15, Getty Images/AFP/Robyn Beck, 7, MCT/Gary W. Green, 5, ZUMA Press/Paul Bersebach, 19; Shutterstock: Piotr Krzeslak, 1

Note to Parents and Teachers

The Sports Stars set supports national social studies standards related to people, places, and culture. This book describes and illustrates stars of professional basketball. The images support early readers in understanding the text. The repetition of words and phrases helps early readers learn new words. This book also introduces early readers to subject-specific vocabulary words, which are defined in the Glossary section. Early readers may need assistance to read some words and to use the Table of Contents, Glossary, Read More, Internet Sites, and Index sections of the book.

Printed in China by Nordica.
1013/CA21301922
092013   007747NORDS14

 Table of Contents

Court Stars

The shot goes up. Swish!
Fans enjoy watching their
favorite basketball stars
in action.

Guards

Kobe Bryant is an NBA great. He has won five NBA titles with the Los Angeles Lakers. He has played in 15 All-Star Games.

NBA stands for National Basketball Association.

Point guard Chris Paul does it all. He can shoot and pass. He's also a top defender. Paul has led the NBA in steals five times.

Forwards

Kevin Durant is a top scorer. He shoots from anywhere on the court. Durant led the NBA in scoring three seasons in a row.

Fans cheer for Blake Griffin's slam dunks. Griffin is a powerful scorer and rebounder. He was named the NBA's top rookie in his first season.

LeBron James is skilled on both ends of the court. He can score and defend. James led the Miami Heat to two NBA titles.

Maya Moore is a champion. She led the Minnesota Lynx to two WNBA titles. She also won an Olympic gold medal with the U.S. women's basketball team.

WNBA stands for Women's National Basketball Association.

Centers

Dwight Howard is a star center.

He works hard to grab rebounds.

Howard has led the NBA in

rebounding five times.

Tina Charles is the WNBA's best center. She blocks shots and gets rebounds. Charles was named the WNBA's MVP in just her third season.

MVP stands for Most Valuable Player.

Glossary

center—the player who usually plays closest to the basket

champion—a person who has won a contest or competition

defend—to try to keep someone from scoring

forward—a player who usually plays close to the basket; forwards often focus on rebounding and blocking shots

guard—a player who frequently handles the ball and often plays mostly outside; guards often focus on passing and shooting

point guard—the player who usually handles the ball and runs a team's offensive plays

rebound—to get the basketball after a shot is missed

rookie—a player in his or her first season on a professional team

slam dunk—a shot in which a player shoves the ball down through the basket

steal—a play in which a defensive player takes the ball away from an offensive player

Read More

Doeden, Matt. *The Best of Pro Basketball*. Best of Pro Sports. Mankato, Minn.: Capstone Press, 2010.

Ladewski, Paul. *Stars on the Court*. New York: Scholastic Inc., 2009.

Savage, Jeff. *LeBron James*. Amazing Athletes. Minneapolis: Lerner Publications Company, 2012.

Internet Sites

FactHound offers a safe, fun way to find Internet sites related to this book. All of the sites on FactHound have been researched by our staff.

Here's all you do:

Visit *www.facthound.com*

Type in this code: 9781476539591

Super-cool stuff! Check out projects, games and lots more at **www.capstonekids.com**

23

Index

Word Count: 209
Grade: 1
Early-Intervention Level: 18